THE VOTE

THAT

MADE THE PRESIDENT.

BY

DAVID DUDLEY FIELD.

NEW YORK:
D. APPLETON & COMPANY,
549 & 551 BROADWAY.
1877.

THE VOTE THAT MADE THE PRESIDENT.

At ten minutes past four o'clock on the second morning of the present month (March, 1877), the President of the Senate of the United States, in the presence of the two Houses of Congress, made this announcement: "The whole number of the electors appointed to vote for President and Vice-President of the United States is 369, of which a majority is 185. The state of the vote for President of the United States, as delivered by the tellers, and as determined under the act of Congress, approved January 29, 1877, on this subject, is: for Rutherford B. Hayes, of Ohio, 185 votes; for Samuel J. Tilden, of New York, 184 votes;" and then, after mentioning the votes for Vice-President, he proceeded: "Wherefore I do declare, that Rutherford B. Hayes, of Ohio, having received a majority of the whole number of electoral votes, is duly elected President of the United States for four years, commencing on the fourth day of March, 1877."

Mr. Hayes was thus declared elected by a majority of one. If any vote counted for him had been counted on the other side, Mr. Tilden, instead of Mr. Hayes, would have had the 185 votes; if it had been rejected altogether, each would have had 184 votes, and the House of Representatives would immediately have elected Mr. Tilden. One vote, therefore, put Mr. Hayes into the presidential office.

To make up the 185 votes counted for him, 8 came from Louisiana and 4 from Florida. Whether they should have been thus counted is a question that affects the honor, the conscience, and the interests of the American people. There is not a person living in this country who has not a direct concern in a just answer. Not one will ever live in it whose respect for this generation will not depend in some degree upon that answer.

The 12 votes were not all alike. Some had one distinction, some another. But, not to distract attention by the discussion of several transactions instead of one, and because one in the present instance actually determined the result, I will confine my observations to a single vote. For this purpose let us take one of the votes from Louisiana, that, for instance, of Orlando H. Brewster.

Brewster was not appointed an elector, inasmuch as he did not receive a majority of the votes cast by the people of Louisiana, and inasmuch also as he could not have been appointed if he had received them all.

He did not receive a Majority of the Votes.

It would be a waste of time and patience to go through the testimony taken by the two Houses of Congress for their own information, before they consented to call in the advice of the Electoral Commission. The evidence of wrongs on both sides, and the irreconcilable contradictions of witnesses, made President Seelye and Mr. Pierce, of Massachusetts, declare it to be impossible for them to reach a satisfactory conclusion upon the facts, and compelled them to break away from their party, and refuse to abide by the advice of the Commission. There are certain things, however, which we know beyond dispute, or about which there is and can be no controversy, and these only will I mention. We know that the number of votes cast in Louisiana for the Tilden electors, taking the first name on the list as representing all, was 83,723, but that the certificate of the Returning Board put them at 70,508, turning Mr. Tilden's majority of more than 6,000 into a majority for Mr. Hayes; and we know that the reduction was made by throwing out more than 13,000 votes of legal voters voting legally for Mr. Tilden, and that more than 10,000 of these were thrown out upon the assumed authority of a statute of Louisiana, which in terms gave the board power to throw out votes, upon examination and deliberation, "whenever, from any poll or voting-place, there shall be received the *statement of any supervisor* of registration *or commissioner* of election, in form as required by section 26 of this act, *on affidavit of three or more citizens*, of any riot, tumult, acts of violence, intimidation, armed disturbance, bribery, or corrupt influences, which prevented, or tended to prevent, a fair, free, and peaceable vote of all qualified electors entitled to vote at such poll or voting-place."

Whether the statute itself has its warrant in the Constitution is a question not necessary now to be considered. For my part, I cannot see the authority for taking out of the ballot-boxes the ballots of lawful voters and throwing them away because other voters did not vote, whatever may have been the cause of their not voting, whether they were frightened, foolish, or perverse. I cannot for the life of me perceive that the State can be held to have elected persons whom it did not in fact elect, because it is conjectured, or even made probable, that if voters who kept away from the polls had in fact attended and voted, they would have made a majority for these persons.

Without going into that question, however, and assuming for the sake of the argument that the statute had all the authority of the most clearly valid statute that was ever passed, it is certain that the only ground upon which a vote could have been thrown out, for intimidation or other corrupt influence, was the statement of a supervisor of registration or commissioner of election, founded upon the affidavits of three citizens. When, however, the vote of Louisiana was before the Electoral Commission, the following offer was made by counsel:

"We offer to prove that *the statements and affidavits* purporting to have been made and forwarded to said Returning Board in pursuance of the provisions of section 26, of the election law of 1872, alleging riot, tumult, intimidation, and violence, at or near certain polls, and in certain parishes, *were* falsely fabricated and *forged* by certain disreputable persons *under the direction*, and with the knowledge, *of said Returning Board*, and that said Returning Board, knowing said statements and affidavits to be false and forged, and that none of the said statements or affidavits were made in the manner or form or within the time required by law, did knowingly, willfully, and fraudulently, fail and refuse to canvass or compile more than 10,000 votes lawfully cast. as is shown by the statements of votes of the Commissioners of Election."

This offer the Commission rejected by a vote of 8 to 7.

In the Commission Mr. Abbott moved the following:

"*Resolved*, That testimony tending to show that the so-called Returning Board of Louisiana had no jurisdiction to canvass the votes for electors of President and Vice-President is admissible."

This was rejected by the same vote.

In explaining the reason of their decision in the case, the Commission used the following language:

"And the Commission has, by a majority of votes, decided, and does hereby decide, that it is not competent, under the Constitution and the law as it existed at the date of the passage of said act, to go into evidence *aliunde*, the papers opened by the President of the Senate, in the presence of the two Houses, to prove that other persons than those regularly certified to by the Governor of the State of Louisiana, on and according to the determination and declaration of their appointment by the returning officers for elections in the said State prior to the time required for the performance of their duties, had been appointed electors, or by counter-proof to show that they had not; or that the determination of the said returning officers was not in accordance with the truth and the fact, the Commission, by a majority of votes, being of opinion that it is not within the jurisdiction of the two Houses of Congress, assembled to count the votes for President and Vice-President, to enter upon a trial of such questions."

Whether, therefore, the decisions of the Commission or the reasons given for them be sound or unsound, it may be assumed, that *Brewster did not receive a majority of the votes cast by the people of Louisiana, and that the action of the Returning Board* in cutting down the majority of his competitor, so as to reduce it below his, *was taken without jurisdiction, and upon the pretense of statements and affidavits which they themselves had caused to be forged.*

Brewster could not have been appointed Elector if he had received the Votes of all the People of Louisiana.

He had been made Surveyor-General of the United States, for the District of Louisiana, on the 2d of February, 1874; was recommissioned by President Grant on the 11th of February, 1875, and is at present exercising the office. Whether he has ever been out of the office depends upon the facts now to be mentioned. Eight or nine days after the election of November 7, 1876, at which he was a candidate on the Republican electoral ticket, there was recived at the Department of the Interior, from the hands of the President, this letter:

Monroe, *November* 4, 1876.

Dear Sir: I hereby tender my resignation of the office of Surveyor-General of the State of Louisiana, with the request that it be accepted immediately. With many thanks for your kindness,

I remain, yours respectfully,
O. H. Brewster.

U. S. Grant, *President United States.*

When the letter was written does not appear. It is certain that Brewster was acting as Surveyor-General on the 10th of November.

On the 16th of November a letter was addressed to the Commissioner of the General Land-Office, as follows:

Department of the Interior,
Washington, *November* 16, 1876.

Sir: I have received the resignation of Mr. Orlando H. Brewster, Surveyor-General of Louisiana, which he has requested may take effect immediately. Please inform Mr. Brewster that his resignation has been accepted by the President, to take effect November 4th instant, that being the date of his letter of resignation to this Department.

Very respectfully,
Z. Chandler, *Secretary.*

At what time, if ever, the Commissioner informed Brewster of the acceptance of his resignation we do not know, but it could not have been earlier than the 20th of November.

On the morning of the 6th of December, the four men who assumed to act as the Returning Board of Louisiana filed in the office of the Secretary of that State a certificate that Brewster, with seven other persons, had been appointed presidential electors. There was then on the statute-book of Louisiana this enactment:

"If any one or more of the electors chosen by the people shall fail from any cause whatever to attend at the appointed place at the hour of 4 P. M. of the day prescribed for their meeting, it shall be the duty of the other electors immediately to proceed by ballot to fill such vacancy or vacancies."

What Brewster did is thus told by Kellogg, one of the Hayes electors, on his examination at Washington in January:

"*Q.* Did Levissee and Brewster vote at the meeting of electors?

A. I believe they did.

Q. Was not an appointment made for somebody to fill Brewster's place?

A. I believe that that is the case.

. . . .

Q. Who was appointed to fill Brewster's place?

A. Brewster himself.

Q. The same man?

A. The same man.

. . . .

Q. Were you also instructed by these committees (National and Congressional Republican Committees) how to dispose of Brewster and Levissee?

A. My recollection is that some one of the electors had received a letter suggesting that in case of a vacancy or in case of the absence of Levissee and Brewster, they should be chosen in their own places. That is my recollection.

. . . .

Q. And yet they absented themselves from the electoral college, and you filled their vacancies with themselves?

A. They were absent from the college when the college met, and we filled their vacancies by themselves."

Being thus installed, they voted for Mr. Hayes within an hour after they were chosen to fill their own vacancies; and three days afterward Brewster addressed the following letter to the President:

NEW ORLEANS, LOUISIANA, *December* 9, 1876.

SIR: I respectfully apply to be appointed Surveyor-General for the District of Louisiana. Commendations from prominent gentlemen will be submitted to your Excellency to justify the appointment.

I have the honor to remain

Your very obedient servant,

ORLANDO H. BREWSTER.

U. S. GRANT, *President United States, Washington, D. C.*

The reappointment was made on the 5th of January, 1877. The Chief of the Appointment Division in the Interior Department was asked and testified about it as follows:

"*Q.* Who recommended his appointment in January?

A. I think the probability is (although there is no evidence of it) that there was no recommendation, further than his own application to the President.

Q. You do not know of any recommendation?

A. I do not know of any.

Q. There is none on file?

A. There is none on file to the best of my knowledge. There is none on file in the Interior Department."

Who does not perceive the shallow trick by which Brewster pretended to have divested himself of his Federal office that he might vote; only to be reinvested as soon as he had voted?

The letter of resignation, with its false date, and its pretended acceptance, to take effect as of a time past, were evident shams to make it appear that he was not holder of a Federal office when he was elected; his affecting to be absent on the 6th of December, and coming in immediately to fill the vacancy occasioned by his own absence, in order to make it appear that his appointment was made on that 6th of December, instead of the 7th of November, and his barefaced application on the third day thereafter to be reappointed to the Federal office, from which he could not possibly have perfected his resignation before the 20th of November—all these were but so many contrivances to evade the highest enactment known to our civil polity. In the eye of reason and of law, he acted during the whole period under that influence of office which it was the design of the Constitution to prevent, and he

must have entered more thoroughly into the work of his Federal master than if he had not gone through the form of resigning, inasmuch as that placed him, more than before, in his master's power.

Let us now place side by side the commandment of the Constitution and the resolution of the Electoral Commission:

COMMANDMENT.	RESOLUTION.
"*No* Senator or Representative, or *person holding an office of trust or profit under the United States, shall be appointed an elector.*"	"The Commission, by a majority of votes, is also of the opinion that *it is not competent to prove that any of said persons, so appointed electors* as aforesaid, *held an office of trust or profit under the United States at the time when they were appointed*, or that they were ineligible under the laws of the State, or any other matter offered to be proved *aliunde* the said certificates and papers."

It would be unjust to cast upon the Electoral Commission the blame of all the wrong that has been practised in this presidential count. The Commission was but a council of advice, which Congress might have taken or not, as it pleased, the only condition being that, in order to reject it, both Houses must have agreed. The responsibility of the final decision lay, after all, upon Congress, or rather, upon the Senate, which voted throughout to follow the Commission.

The facts thus briefly recited present certain questions—moral, political, and legal—which cannot be considered too soon for our good repute and our self-respect.

The Moral Question.

Whatever differences of opinion there may be about the political and legal questions involved, there can be none about the moral. The presidential office is the gift of the people of the several States, of their own free-will, expressed according to the laws. A falsification of that will is an offense against the State where it is committed, and against all the

States. If the falsification is beyond the reach of the law, it is not beyond the reach of the conscience. A robbery is none the less a robbery because it is beyond the range of vision or the arm of justice. If the possessor of an estate has entered through the forgery of a record or the spoliation of a will, which although believed by every neighbor is beyond judicial proof, all the world pronounces his possession fraudulent, even though he scatters his wealth in charities and gathers many companions around his luxurious table. The example is corrupting, but it is against the eternal law of justice that the act should be respected or the actors continue forever to prosper.

It is no answer to these observations to say that frauds have been practised on the other side. Unhappily there is too much reason to believe that neither party is free from practices which are at once a scourge and a dishonor. Neither has the disgraceful monopoly of such practices, whichever may have the bad preëminence. But this is certain: one wrong neither justifies nor palliates another.

There is no set-off known to the moral law. Because A has defrauded B, that is no reason why B should defraud A. If it were so, society would go on forever in a compound ratio of crime. The first breach of the law would furnish excuse for the second, and their progeny would follow in sad progression to the end of time. This is not, however, the moral condition of the world. The *lex talionis* has been abolished by the law of civilization and the higher law of the gospel.

In this case of Louisiana there can be neither excuse nor palliation for the misconduct of the Returning Board.

On the 10th of November, President Grant telegraphed to the General of the Army instructions about troops in Louisiana and Florida, and added that "*no man worthy of the office of President should be willing to hold it if counted in or placed there by fraud.* Either party can afford to be disappointed in the result. *The country cannot afford to have the result tainted by the suspicion of illegal or false returns.*" And again: "The presence of citizens from other States, I understand, is requested in Louisiana, to see that the Board of Canvassers makes *a fair count of the vote actually cast.* It is to be hoped that representative and fair men of both parties will go."

Did the President of that day misrepresent his party, or his successor, or has the party changed and the successor also? Had the virtuous impulses of November faded away in February? Was there a change of heart or a change of opportunity? Neither Congress nor the Electoral Commission could give an *honest* title, without investigating the honesty of the transactions on which the title was founded; and yet a President has been installed, in the face of rejected offers to prove frauds, the grossest, the most shameless, and the most corrupting, in all our history.

Then what was the object of the committees of each House of Congress, sent into the disputed States? Was it to blind the people? Was it to conceal a meditated fraud? On the very first day of the session, December 4th, Mr. Edmunds, in the Senate, moved certain resolutions, of which this was one:

"*Resolved further*, That the said committee" (the Committee on Privileges and Elections) "be, and is hereby, instructed to inquire into the eligibility to office under the Constitution of the United States of any persons alleged to have been ineligible on the 7th day of November last, or to be ineligible as electors of President and Vice-President of the United States, to whom certificates of election have been, or shall be, issued by the Executive authority of any State, as such electors, and *whether the appointment of electors*, or those claiming to be such, in any of the States, *has been made either by force, fraud, or other means otherwise than in conformity with the Constitution and laws of the United States, and the laws of the respective States;* and whether any such appointment or action of any such elector has been in any wise unconstitutionally or unlawfully interfered with; and to inquire and report whether Congress has any constitutional power, and, if so, what and the extent thereof, in respect of the appointment of or action of electors of President and Vice-President of the United States, or over returns or certificates of votes of such electors," etc.

Was all this parade of committees sent hither and thither, summoning witnesses from far and near, committing the recusant to prison, and looking into State archives; was all this a mock show, a piece of pantomime, for the amusement of the lookers-on, while conspirators were plotting how to conceal what they pretended to be wishing to discover? Taken all in all, the sounding profession, the bustling search, and the studied concealment, make a drama, half comedy and half tragedy, the like of which this generation has not seen till now, but the like of which it and its successors may see many times, if the audience does not hiss the play, and remit the actors to the streets.

It has been objected, as a reason for not receiving offered evidence, that there was not time to take it before the 4th of March. How was that known? Perhaps it could have been taken in an hour. Why was not the question asked, how much time the evidence would take, before it was excluded? If the certificate was false, and the falsehood was susceptible of proof, every effort possible should have been made to receive it, and receive it all. It is not commonly accepted as good reason for not searching after the truth, that the search may be difficult. Nor is it an unusual occurrence to require an argument or decision to be made within a period limited. Ten minutes' speeches in Congress, two hours' argument in the Supreme Court, a jury shut in a room until they agree upon a verdict, a court required by statute to render its decision by a day fixed, are not so strange as to be remarkable, or found in practice so embarrassing as to cause the practice to be abandoned.

Nor is it any answer to say that, if the offer of evidence had been accepted, the proof would have fallen short of the offer. That does not lie in the mouth of any one to say, who excluded the evidence, or justified its exclusion. The characters of the counsel who made the offer, and of the commissioner who moved its acceptance, are a guarantee not only of their good faith, but of a reason for their belief. No man has any right to deny that the proof offered would have been made good, who refused the opportunity. They who closed their ears should in decency keep their mouths shut. But it was not the counsel and the commissioner alone who believed that the proof offered would be made good. Every one who witnessed the examinations in Washington, every one who read the testimony taken by the Congressional Committees in Louisiana, must have been satisfied that the conduct of the

Returning Board was throughout unlawful, wicked, and shocking, to the last degree.

The title of the acting President, however valid in law, if valid at all, is tainted with fraud in fact. There was fraud in certifying that Brewster had received a majority of the votes of Louisiana, and fraud in attempting to evade that part of the Constitution which pronounced his disqualification. When the Electoral Commission advised Congress, and Congress accepted, by not rejecting, the advice, that fraud could not be proved, that advice being but the equivalent of saying that fraud was of no consequence; when it advised that the incompetency of the Returning Board, for want of jurisdiction, could not be proved, such proof being but the equivalent of proof that the pretended board was not a board at all; when it advised that the forgery, by direction of the board, of the statements and affidavits on which it pretended to act as true could not be proved, that proof being but the equivalent of proof that the pretended statements and affidavits were not statements and affidavits at all; when it advised that the barrier raised by the Constitution against the appointment of a Federal officer to choose a Federal President, was not a barrier at all—the moral sense of the whole American people was shocked. No form of words can cover up the falsehood; no sophistry can hide it; no lapse of time wash it out. It will follow its contrivers wherever they go, confront them whenever they turn, and as often as one of them asks the suffrages of his countrymen, he may expect to hear them reply, "Why do you reason with us, why seek to persuade us into giving you our votes, you that have taught us such a contempt for votes, that one fraudulent certificate is better than ten thousand of them?"

The Political Question.

The advice of the Commission, with the consequent action of Congress, was a virtual affirmation of this proposition, that if on the morning of the 6th of December the Federal general commanding in Louisiana had surrounded the State-House with soldiers, and marching in eight of his captains, had compelled the Returning Board to certify their appointment as electors, and the Governor to add his certificate, Congress and the country would have been obliged to accept the votes of these captains as the constitutional and lawful votes of Louisiana electors. Whoever supposes that the union of these States can endure under such an interpretation of their fundamental law, must be endowed with credulity beyond the simplicity of childhood. The doctrine is an open invitation to transgression and usurpation. The judicious disposition of a few troops in the capitals of disputed States, on the day of the electoral vote, will perpetuate an Administration just so long as the audacity of a President, or the cupidity of his office-holders, may find it desirable; unless, indeed, it be found, as is most likely, that the ways of fraud are cheaper, easier, and less palpable than the ways of force.

The Legal Question.

As to the conclusiveness of the Governor's and canvassers' certificates. The doctrine of the majority of the Commission, and of the Senate, is, that the certificate of the Governor "*on and according to the determination and declaration*" of the State canvassers, cannot be shown to be false, though it may have been obtained by force or fraud. This doctrine admits that the truth of the *Governor's* certificate can be inquired into, else why the qualification that it must be "*on and according to*" the canvasser's certificate. It is said to be good only when in such accord; therefore, when not in accord, it is good for nothing. We may, then, dismiss the Governor's certificate as of no account, and to be left therefore out of further discussion. The substance of the doctrine is, that the *certificate of the State canvassers* cannot be contradicted.

This language must, of course, be understood, as used in reference to the question at that time depending; that is to say, whether evidence to contradict or annul the certificate was then and there admissible. It had already been decided in the Florida case that no action of the State authorities, after the electors had voted, could affect the validity of the vote. Whether such action before the vote would have been of any avail was not decided, and will never be decided, unless a radical change is made in the laws, since, according to present legislation, the vote of the electors treads fast on the heels of their appointment. In Florida, they were declared appointed at three o'clock in the morning, and they voted at twelve, just nine hours afterward. In Louisiana the interval was even less. To suppose that any State action would or could be had in such an interval, or in any interval possible under present laws, would be as wild as to suppose that counting in a President by fraud will not be followed by imitators at future elections.

Taking the doctrine, however, precisely as it was applied in the instance of Louisiana, it is this: that the certificate of State canvassers cannot be impeached by evidence showing either that they had no jurisdiction to canvass the electoral vote at all, or that they had no jurisdiction to throw away votes that were actually cast, inasmuch as the power to throw away came into existence only when affidavits were laid before them, and there were no affidavits except such as they had caused to be forged, which, in the eye of the law, were not affidavits at all.

One would say that such a doctrine, held up in its nakedness, need hardly be attacked, for no man, not maddened by the fanaticism of party, would be found willing to defend it; yet if not defended, the disposition of the Louisiana case must be pronounced as unsound in law as it was injurious in policy and offensive in morals. But I go further, and deny the conclusiveness of the canvassers' certificate under any circumstances. Suppose the question to be put thus: Can the certificate of State canvassers, acting within the scope of their authority, be questioned by evidence of mistake, fraud, or duress; what should be the answer? Most certainly it can, should be answered.

The statutes of the State may or may not have declared the effect of the certificate. In the case of Louisiana, this was the only statute relevant:

"The returns of the elections thus made and promulgated shall be *prima-facie* evidence in all courts of justice and before all civil officers, until set aside after a contest according to law, of the right of any person named therein to hold and exercise the office to which he shall by such return be declared elected."

Whatever doubt may have been expressed or felt whether this statute applied to the canvassers of a presidential election, or whether the words *prima facie* really meant *prima facie*, or whether "courts of justice," and "civil officers," included the Electoral Commission and the two Houses of Congress, there can be no doubt that "the returns of the elections thus made and promulgated" do not include returns canvassed without jurisdiction, or made under cover of pretended affidavits which the returning officers themselves caused to be forged.

But, passing from this view of the subject, although this is sufficient to dispose of Brewster's pretensions, let us suppose a stronger case—the strongest supposable—that of a State Legislature directing not only the manner in which electors shall be appointed, but directing also that the certificate of the State canvassers shall be conclusive evidence that the State has appointed in the manner directed.

Because the Constitution provides that electors shall be appointed by the State, in the manner directed by its Legislature, it is thence inferred that the State must furnish the evidence of the appointment, and of course that none can be received except that which the State has furnished. And this is said to be the true States-rights doctrine. It is a strange sight, that of gentlemen clamoring for State rights who will not allow the people of Louisiana and South Carolina to take care of themselves; who are even now debating at Washington whether they shall not order new elections in those States, or which of two State governments they shall put up and which put down, and who since the war have treated the South as if no States were there, parceling it into military districts, and denying recognition until constitutional amendments were ratified. Their assertion of the conclusiveness of false and fraudulent canvassers' certificates, on the pretense of upholding State rights, should seem to be thrown in our faces by way of bravado, unless it be meant, indeed, for burlesque masking hypocrisy. But if the sight were not strange, and those gentlemen had been all along as careful of the rights of the States as they are of their own places, there is nothing in the claim for the conclusiveness of canvassers' certificates which receives support from the doctrine of State rights. On the contrary, the rights of the States are best preserved by fencing them against force or fraud, by leaving them untrammeled in their own action, and leaving us untrammeled in finding out what that action has been. No rights are ever lost by letting in the light.

A certificate can be conclusive evidence of the States' action, only when the act and the certificate are identical. If the Constitution had provided that there should be sent from each State a certificate signed by such persons as the Legislature might designate, declaring who should cast the electoral votes, then the only inquiry that could have been made at Washington would have been, whether the certificate sent up was so signed and the persons therein mentioned had voted; but the Constitution has provided nothing of the kind. It has provided that the State shall appoint in the manner directed by its Legislature, and the inquiry thereupon to be made at the Capitol is, "Whom has the State appointed in the manner directed?"

We agree that the State has complete power, within certain limits regarding the persons who may be appointed, to appoint its electors in any manner its Legislature may direct, but whether the State has done so is open to inquiry. Canvassers of votes are not the State, or the Legislature of the State, and their certificate is nothing but evidence. Two facts are to be shown: one that the State has acted, and the other that the act has been in conformity to the directions of the Legislature. There is nothing in positive law, or in the reason of things, which, if the fact certified do not exist, requires that its falsity should not be open to proof.

The Electoral Commission and the Senate read the Constitution as if the words following in italics were part of it:

"Each State shall appoint, in such manner as the Legislature thereof may direct, a number of electors equal to the whole number of Senators and Representatives to which the State may be entitled in the Congress; but no Senator or Representative, or person holding an office of trust or profit under the United States, shall be appointed an elector." *And the certificate of such officers as the Legislature of the State may designate shall be conclusive evidence, not only that the persons certified were appointed by the State, but that they were appointed in the manner directed by its Legislature, any mistake, fraud, or duress, of the certifying officers to the contrary notwithstanding.*

But the words of the Constitution as they stand do not carry with them the words in italics, or their substance; and if it had been proposed to add them when the Constitution was presented to the people, I do not believe that they would have been accepted.

Had it been suggested to the freemen of Massachusetts or Connecticut that they should give to the Legislature of another State not only the right of designating how the electors should be chosen, whose voices might make a President for them, but also the right to designate a permanent board, with power to say, in the face of the truth, who had or had not been chosen, the voices of John Hancock and Oliver Ellsworth would surely have warned the good people of their native Commonwealths against so dangerous a proposition.

There is no necessary connection between an appointment and the certificate of it, unless the two acts are performed by the same persons. If the appointment of electors for Louisiana had been committed to the Returning Board, then there might be reason for saying that the certificate was conclusive, because they appointed when they certified. But the board had not the power of appointment. That power could not have been given to them, if the Legislature of Louisiana had so intended, and it did not so intend.

The power to give a conclusive certificate of appointment —that is, a certificate that precludes further inquiry—is virtually a power to appoint, since no one is then permitted to go behind the certificate to show that there was neither valid appointment nor form of appointment. Unless, therefore, the Legislature of Louisiana could, under the Constitution, confer upon the Returning Board power to appoint presidential electors for Louisiana, it could not confer upon it power to give a conclusive certificate of appointment. The constitution of this Returning Board is known to us all. It was a permanent body, holding for an undefined period, or for life, consisting of four persons of one party, when there should have been five, of different parties; and the four had persistently refused for years to select a fifth. To pretend that such a body was, or could lawfully be, empowered to appoint eight electors for the people of Louisiana, to match the eight who were appointed by the people of Maryland, would be simple effrontery; and most certainly, as I have said, if they could not appoint, they could not give an incontrovertible certificate of appointment. The certificate is one thing; the appointment another. The State appoints and the Legislature directs the manner of appointment, but neither can make true that which is false.

Now as to the person appointed. Brewster was one of the very persons sought to be excluded by these words of the Constitution: "No Senator or Representative, or person holding an office of trust or profit under the United States, shall be appointed an elector." He was, nevertheless, appointed, and he voted, and his vote made the President. How was this brought about? The Commission answer, "That it is not competent to prove that any of said persons so appointed electors as aforesaid held an office of trust or profit under the United States at the time when they were appointed." Of course, if it was not competent to prove it, the fact itself must have been of no importance.

Bentham's "Book of Fallacies" may be enriched, in another edition, with another fallacy, as remarkable as any he has recorded, to wit, that prohibition in the American Constitution means prohibition! Talleyrand was once asked the meaning of non-intervention. "Non-intervention," he replied, "non-intervention means about the same thing as intervention." So, in our new constitutional vocabulary, prohibition means about the same thing as permission.

It was, indeed, mentioned in the course of the argument, though the Commission does not appear to have thought much of it, that Brewster, having resigned his Federal office, and come in upon a new appointment, to fill his own vacant place on the 6th of December, being then both present and absent, the question of eligibility did not arise. But enough has been said about this resignation sham. If such a trick had been played in respect to a note-of-hand of five dollars, there is not a justice of the peace who would not have denounced the trick, as conferring no right and affording no protection.

The people of New York were amused, three or four years ago, with the feats of a juggler, who dressed one side of him as a man, and the other as a woman, and who turned about so quickly that he showed himself as two persons of different sexes in the same instant. Brewster's feat was not less remarkable: he was at once absent and present; absent that he might be appointed, and present that he might vote; went through the whole performance in less than an hour, absenting himself that he might be called in to be present, presenting himself though absent, voting ballots and signing certificates, showing himself to be as versatile and as agile as that master of jugglery.

Upon what theory the Commission held that evidence could not be received of Brewster's Federal office at the time of his appointment does not appear. He certainly was in the prohibited category. A marriage between persons within prohibited degrees is not good, even if consummated. The prohibited union of two offices in the same person should not be thought a legal union, simply because it is practised. It has been said, though the Commission did not say it, that Brewster was at least elector *de facto*, and his vote was good, whatever may have been his title. Then why should we trouble ourselves about the returning officer's certificate? If, as elector *de facto*, his vote was good, then it was good without the certificate, and all that the Commission should have looked into was the *fact of voting*, without troubling themselves about the certificate of anybody or any other evidence of title. But, in truth, the distinctions between officers *de facto* and officers *de jure* have no application to the present case, and for this reason, among others, that two persons cannot hold the same office *de facto*. It is of the essence of a *de-facto* possession of office that it should be exclusive. The Chancellor of New York said, in a judicial opinion, more than thirty years ago: "When there is but one office there cannot be an officer *de jure* and an officer *de facto* both in possession of the office at the same time." This is true even when the

office is a continuing one. Who, for instance, can say which of the rival Governors in Louisiana or South Carolina at this moment is the Governor *de facto?* In deciding between them, would not all the world pronounce this the only question, which is Governor *de jure?* Much more is it true when the office is temporary, existing but for a moment, even if the doctrine of a *de-facto* officer can be applied to such an office at all. In the present case, Brewster went into the State-House and voted for Mr. Hayes; at the same instant his rival went into the same State-House and voted for Mr. Tilden. It is absurd to pronounce Brewster, under such circumstances, an elector *de facto*, so as to make his vote for that reason good against his rival in the Tilden college, who was as much an elector *de facto* as was Brewster, and had this difference in his favor, that he was elected, and was eligible, while Brewster, the intruder, was not eligible, and was not elected. The only returns which went to the Electoral Commission were the double ones, where rival colleges of electors had acted at the same time in the same State. In those cases, as already observed, the question of a *de-facto* elector could not arise. There was but one case, that of Wisconsin, where it could have arisen, and in that there was but a single return, which, of course, did not go to the Commission.

Conclusion.

Although these pages have been occupied with the vote of Brewster in the electoral college, it should not be understood, that the other seven votes which were counted from that State, and the four votes counted from Florida, were any better than his. The one here considered had its peculiarities; the others had theirs. All of them were tainted, and the counting in of the President *de facto* was twelve times fraudulent. What may be the outcome I do not know. That will depend upon the spirit of this generation and the spirit of those to follow. It is a consolation to know that the questions will be reviewed by a tribunal higher than the Electoral Commission, higher even than the two Houses of Congress—the American people—from whose judgment there is no appeal but to the final judgment of history.

New York, *March* 28, 1877.

www.ingramcontent.com/pod-product-compliance
Lightning Source LLC
LaVergne TN
LVHW011142110826
845150LV00008B/2461
* 9 7 8 1 4 1 8 1 9 2 6 0 0 *